7/13
3.4

"Exploring the Earth and Beyond"
Funding for this item provided by a
Library Services and Technology (LSTA)
Grant made possible by the Illinois
State Library - 2013

Giant Pandas

by Molly Kolpin

Consultant:
Frank T. van Manen
Research Ecologist
U.S. Geological Survey
Leetown Science Center

CAPSTONE PRESS
a capstone imprint

First Facts is published by Capstone Press,
1710 Roe Crest Drive, North Mankato, Minnesota 56003.
www.capstonepub.com

Books published by Capstone Press are manufactured with paper
containing at least 10 percent post-consumer waste.

Library of Congress Cataloging-in-Publication Data
Kolpin, Molly.
 Giant pandas / by Molly Kolpin.
   p. cm. — (First facts. Bears)
 Includes bibliographical references and index.
 Summary: "Discusses giant panda bears, including their physical features, habitat,
range, and life cycle"—Provided by publisher.
 ISBN 978-1-4296-6132-4 (library binding)
 ISBN 978-1-4296-7185-9 (paperback)
 1. Giant panda—Juvenile literature. I. Title. II. Series.
 QL737.C27K649 2012
 599.789—dc22   2011001585

Editorial Credits
Christine Peterson, editor; Kyle Grenz, designer; Laura Manthe, production specialist

Photo Credits
Alamy: blickwinkel/McPHOTO/LAY, 21, blickwinkel/Poelking, 10, Elvele Images
Ltd/Fritz Poelking, 13, Keren Su/China Span, 9, Natural Visions/Heather Angel, 7,
Steve Bloom Images, 16; Digital Vision, cover; Getty Images Inc.: Aurora/C.S. Ling,
5, Photographer's Choice/Daniel J Cox, 15, Photographer's Choice/Gary Vestal, 19;
Shutterstock: fenghui, 20, Kitch Bain, 1

Artistic Effects
Shutterstock: Andrejs Pidjass, jstan

Essential content terms are **bold** and are defined at the bottom of the spread where they
first appear.

Printed in the United States of America in North Mankato, Minnesota.
012012   006536CGVMI

Table of Contents

Famous Bears

Giant pandas are famous for their black and white coats. But they are also symbols of wildlife **conservation**.

Male pandas can weigh 275 pounds (125 kilograms), but females are smaller. Males can be 4 to 6 feet (1.2 to 1.8 meters) long. Pandas have strong jaws. Their wide, flat teeth are made to crush and chew **bamboo**.

Fact!
Giant pandas are the rarest of all the world's bears.

conservation—the protection of animals and plants
bamboo—a tall grass with a hard, hollow stem

5

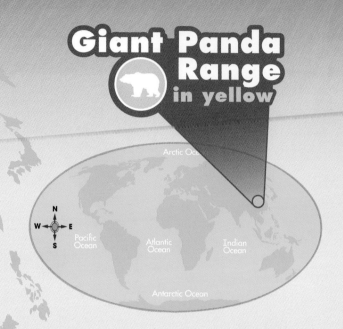

Arctic Oce

Pacific
Ocean

Atlantic
Ocean

Indian
Ocean

Antarctic Ocean

N
W E
S

At Home in China

Giant pandas live in the mountains
of central China. They make their
homes in cool, rainy forests.

About 1,600 pandas live in the world.
Many bears have lost their homes to
farms and logging. Giant pandas are
endangered. Today laws help protect
their homes.

endangered—at risk of dying out

Green Eaters

To keep up their size, giant pandas spend 12 hours a day eating. They eat 30 to 40 pounds (14 to 18 kg) of bamboo each day. Pandas first pull off the bamboo leaves and swallow them. Then they chomp off pieces of stem.

Fact!

Giant pandas may wander up or down a mountain in search of food.

teeth

9

A Panda's Day

Giant pandas drink from rivers and streams running down mountainsides. When pandas aren't eating or drinking, they sit high up in trees. They curl up on the ground or lean on a tree's trunk to sleep.

Fact!
Pandas are skilled swimmers.

A Winter Coat

When cold weather hits, some bears **hibernate**. But giant pandas are active all year long. Their short, thick fur keeps them warm through the winter. Their oily fur also keeps their skin dry during rain and snow.

Fact!
Some pandas have white and brown fur instead of white and black.

hibernate—to spend the winter in a deep sleep

Preparing for Cubs

Male and female giant pandas **mate** in the spring. By August or September, female pandas are ready to give birth. But first they must find a den where their newborn cubs will be safe. Most pandas make their dens in hollow trees or caves.

Fact!
Some female pandas cover their dens with branches and sticks to make it hard for other animals to find.

mate—to join together to produce young

Life Cycle of a Giant Panda

Newborn—At birth, panda cubs are blind and have little hair.

Young—Pandas stay with their mothers until age 2 or 3.

panda cub

Adult—Giant pandas are adults at age 6.

Just Starting Out

A female panda gives birth in her den. Giant pandas often give birth to twins. But usually only one cub survives. Newborn cubs weigh 3 to 5 ounces (85 to 142 grams).

A mother panda cradles her cub in her paw. She holds it close to her body. For two or three weeks, the mother panda doesn't leave her cub, not even to eat.

Becoming Adults

Young pandas learn to stay safe in the forest. They climb trees to escape from enemies. They learn to watch out for **predators**. By age 3, pandas live on their own. Giant pandas are adults at age 6. In the wild, giant pandas can live for more than 20 years.

Fact!
About 300 giant pandas live in zoos.

predator—an animal that hunts another animal for food

Protecting Pandas

People are the greatest threat to giant pandas. People destroy pandas' **habitats** to build farms, homes, and roads. Laws help protect pandas and their homes.

habitat—the place and natural conditions in which an animal lives

Amazing but True!

Pandas have an extra-long wrist bone. The wrist bone is covered with skin and acts like a thumb. This "thumb" helps giant pandas hold a bamboo plant's skinny stem.

Glossary

bamboo (bam-BOO)—a tall grass with a hard, hollow stem

conservation (kon-sur-VAY-shuhn)—the protection of animals and plants

endangered (in-DAYN-juhrd)—at risk of dying out

habitat (HAB-uh-tat)—the place and natural conditions in which an animal lives

hibernate (HYE-bur-nate)—to spend winter in a deep sleep

mate (MEYT)—to join together to produce young

predator (PRED-uh-ter)—an animal that hunts other animals for food

Read More

Greve, Tom. *Giant Pandas*. Eye to Eye with Endangered Species. Vero Beach, Fla.: Rourke Pub., 2011.

Keller, Susanna. *Meet the Panda*. At the Zoo. New York: PowerKids Press, 2010.

Star, Fleur, and Lorrie Mack. *Watch Me Grow Panda*. Watch Me Grow. New York: DK Pub., 2008.

Internet Sites

FactHound offers a safe, fun way to find Internet sites related to this book. All of the sites on FactHound have been researched by our staff.

Here's all you do:

Visit *www.facthound.com*

Type in this code: 9781429661324

Check out projects, games and lots more at **www.capstonekids.com**

Index